S0-BYW-414

WOMAN,
THOU ART
LOOSED!

workbook

WOMAN, THOU ART LOOSED!

T.D. Jakes

workbook

TREASURE HOUSE
An Imprint of
DESTINY IMAGE® PUBLISHERS, INC.
P.O. Box 310, Shippensburg, PA 17257-0310

"For where your treasure is, there will your heart be also." Matthew 6:21

This book and all other Destiny Image, Revival Press, MercyPlace, Fresh Bread, Destiny Image Fiction, and Treasure House books are available at Christian bookstores and distributors worldwide.

To place a book order, call toll-free: **1-800-722-6774.**

For more information on foreign distributors, call **717-532-3040.**

Or reach us on the Internet: **www.destinyimage.com**

ISBN 10: 0-7684-2404-6
ISBN 13: 978-0-7684-2404-1

For Worldwide Distribution, Printed in the U.S.A.

25 26 27 28 29 30 / 10 09 08 07 06

CONTENTS

HOW TO USE THIS STUDY GUIDE

This study guide has been uniquely prepared for the adult learner for personal or small group learning. As such, questions have been developed to allow you or your group time for discussion and application for spiritual growth. In light of this, it is receommended that you follow these guidelines:

Become aware of the book, *Woman, Thou Art Loosed!* Start with the Contents page and then familiarize yourself with the titles and subjects of each chapter.

Have your Bible, the book *Woman, Thou Art Loosed!*, and the Workbook together with pen and pencil. Since satan would love to keep you from your growth in God, eliminate as many distractions as possible.

Read each chapter, looking up any Scriptures not written out in the book. Further, you are encouraged to use a concordance to check other Scriptures that relate to the ones being studied. Doing this can increase your depth of knowledge and understanding.

Answer the questions as provided in the Workbook to the best of your ability. Your personal answers can be shared with others at your discretion. However, sharing with and listening to others can increase your understanding as you struggle together with the concepts in the book and in God's Word.

I hope and pray that you will greatly benefit from the learning process, and that you will use the knowledge you gain for the Kingdom of God.

chapter

1

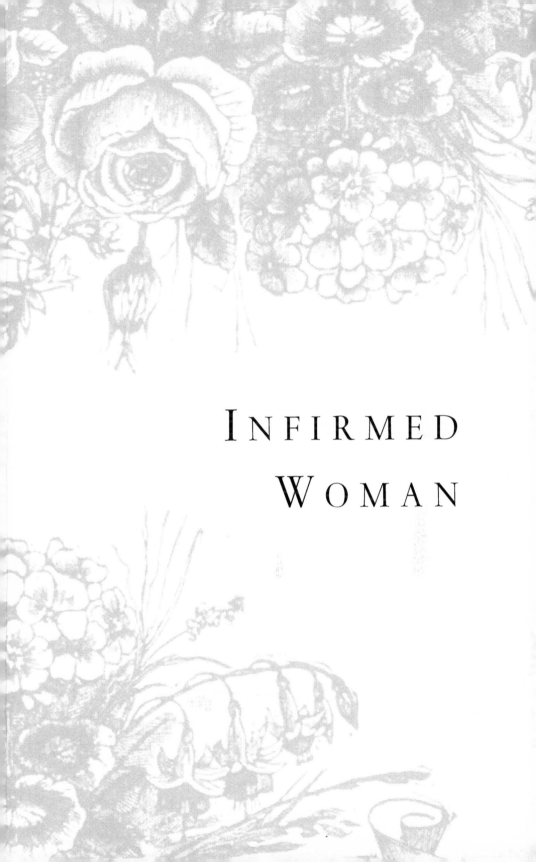

INFIRMED
WOMAN

~ 1 ~

A. What are the three main characters in the account of the infirmed woman in Luke 13:11-12?

B. How do these characters relate to each other?

~ 2 ~

What is the prescription for any problem, even those rooted in the past? Explain using Scripture.

15

~ 3 ~

When Jesus "loosed" the woman, He spoke to the femininity of women. Discuss the importance of this action in light of today's society.

16

~ 4 ~

True or False. An emotional infirmity can be just as difficult to deal with as a physical infirmity.

~ 5 ~

A. When a person is hurting, how does she tend to use other people?

B. What are the problems of doing this?

17

~ 6 ~

True or False. An infirmed woman always lacks effort and fortitude.

~ 7 ~

What was the root of the disappointment and depression in the life of this woman in Luke 13:11-12?

18

~ 8 ~

One of the great heal-
ing balms of the Holy Spirit
is _____.

~ 9 ~

Is there anyone in
your life whom you need to
forgive—including your-
self? Take a moment and
express your forgiveness
for yourself and for that
other person.

~ 10 ~

How can a person, damaged by her life's events, be completely transformed into a whole woman?

~ 11 ~

Discuss the grace and truth found in Jesus' statement, "Woman, thou art loosed."

~ 12 ~

Discuss male/female relations in the light of uniqueness and unity.

~ 13 ~

A. By nature a woman is a
   _____.

B. What are the spiritual
   aspects of that truth?

~ 14 ~

Explain this principle: Forgetting isn't a memory lapse; it is a memory release.

24

Further Challenge: Follow through on the book's suggestion to write down 30 things you would like to do with your life. Then check them off, one by one, as you accomplish them!

chapter

2

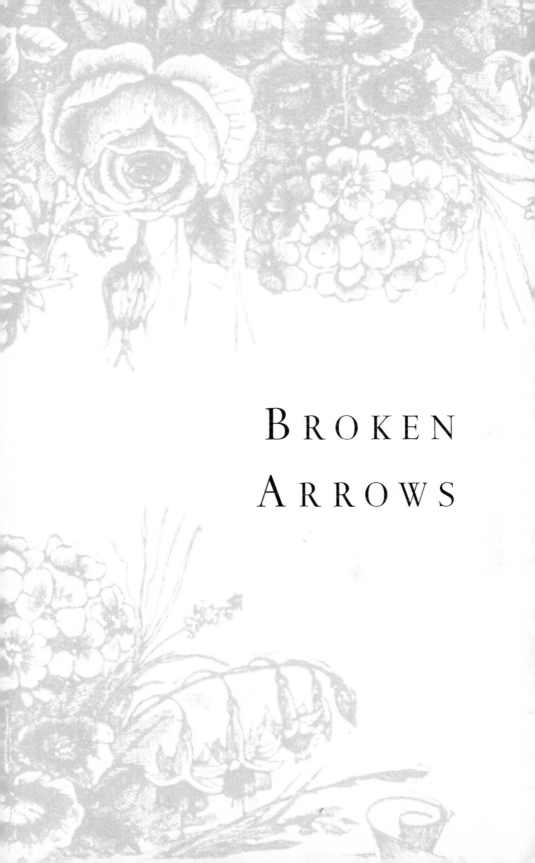

BROKEN
ARROWS

~ 1 ~

Why did the psalmist David compare children to arrows (Ps. 127:3-5)?

~ 2 ~

How would you
describe a broken arrow?

~ 3 ~

A. Compassion is _____ _____ _____.

B. How does compassion relate to healing? Explain using Scripture.

~ 4 ~

Is pain prejudiced?
Explain.

~ 5 ~

People have their own stories. Share (as you can) about any broken arrows in your life whom you've been able to touch.

~ 6 ~

A. Describe how Jesus ministered to the children brought to Him.

B. How does this challenge you in your life?

~ 7 ~

A. Salvation is _____

_____

_____

_____.

B. In what ways can you yourself be like a child in God's presence?

~ 8 ~

Would you consider the pulling of misery from a memory as an event or as a process? Explain your reasoning.

~ 9 ~

Think of a time when you experienced the security of God's arms. Describe how you felt. What did it do for you?

36

~ 10 ~

A. What does it mean to be uncovered?

B. How does God cover His people?

~ 11 ~

For the hurting, God has _____.

~ 12 ~

Describe a time when God brought you or a family member through a crisis.

Further Challenge: List some specific ways that you and your church can become more compassionate care givers to the "broken arrows" around you. Meet with your pastor and discuss the possibility of implementing some of these ideas.

39

chapter

3

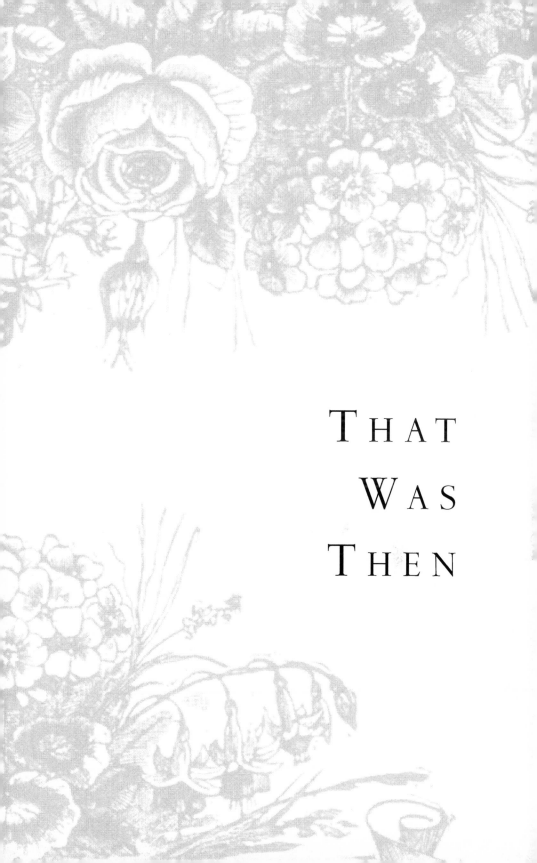

THAT WAS THEN

~ 1 ~

Describe some of your
own spiritual "beginnings."

~ *2* ~

In striving for holiness, what were people actually trying to perfect?

~ 3 ~

How do you achieve holiness?

~ 4 ~

Describe the function of the Church in relation to caring for "people with a past."

~ 5 ~

A. Using the examples in the book or of people whom you know, describe some "people with a past."

B. How can you respond to a "person with a past"?

~ 6 ~

We must maintain a strong line of _____ between a person's _____ and _____.

~ 7 ~

What was it that Jesus understood about meeting people?

~ 8 ~

The chains that bind are often _____.

~ 9 ~

Some chains can be from willfully _____
_____
_____
_____.

~ 10 ~

What three things does Jesus come to do for the hurting?

~ 11 ~

What can women find
as a result of Jesus' power
operating in their lives?

Further Challenge: Name some things that keep the Church from accepting people with brokenness in their lives. What can be done to break down these barriers? Consider yourself as well, and begin to knock down the barriers you find in yourself.

50

chapter

4

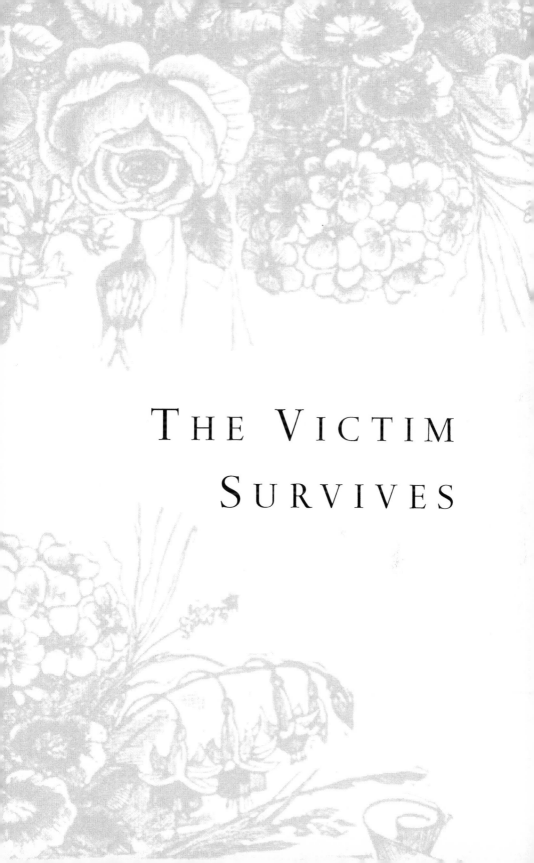

THE VICTIM
SURVIVES

~ 1 ~

How does David's life show that children are most vulnerable to their father's weaknesses? Can you think of other biblical examples?

~ *2* ~

What is the difference
between love and lust?

~ 3 ~

What kind of healing does Jesus want to give?

~ 4 ~

A. What is a tendency women have that makes them vulnerable to abuse?

B. How can women safeguard themselves against falling into traps?

~ 5 ~

True or False. It is not your fault if you are being abused by being made a victim, but it is your fault if you don't allow God's Word to arrest sin and weakness in your life.

~ 6 ~

What are some ways God provides for healing and filling a woman's need for godly self-esteem and acceptance?

~ 7 ~

God's people are to
_____ and
_____ one
another.

~ 8 ~

What does the state-
ment "Love embraces the
totality of the other person"
mean to you?

~ 9 ~

A. What is the secret to being transformed from a victim to a victor?

B. How can the Church be part of this process? Explain using Scripture.

C. Consider this process in light of your personal experience. How has the Lord transformed you?

Further Challenge: List the characteristics of a person you could really open up to and who would help you go through the healing process. Are you yourself such a person? If you would like to be, in what areas do you need to mature? If you are a victim, do you know such a person you could go to? Be encouraged to open yourself up to the healing process.

62

chapter

5

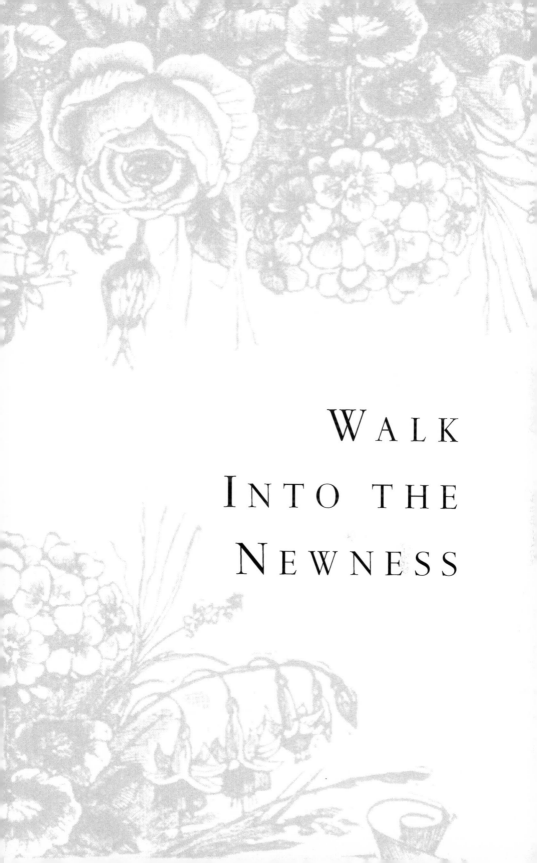

WALK
INTO THE
NEWNESS

~ 1 ~

Have you ever had any-
thing happen to you that
changed you forever?
Describe the change.

66

~ 2 ~

What abuse did Amnon do to Tamar that was worse than rape?

~ 3 ~

The call of the Spirit to those feeling unwanted is
" _____."

~ 4 ~

Describe how Jesus ministered to the infirmed woman of Luke 13:11-12.

~ 5 ~

Describe how standing up and living in the "now" of life is part of the recovery process.

~ 6 ~

It is Jesus'_____ and _____ that touches and heals the hurting places in a woman's life.

~ 7 ~

What else does God restore to your soul when He declares your freedom?

~ *8* ~

What things should the Church, the Body of Christ, be providing for the hurting?

~ 9 ~

A. List the three tenses of faith. What does each of these mean to you?

B. Which of these is the most important, and why?

Further Challenge: Instead of focusing on the tragedies of your life, focus on the victories. Make a list of the things you can praise God for, amidst the troubles in your life. Then actively praise God for them.

chapter

6

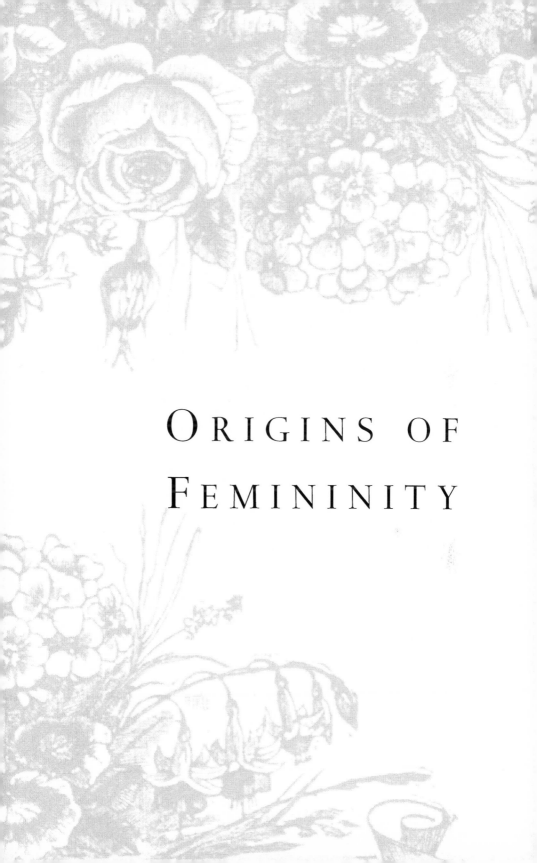

ORIGINS OF FEMININITY

~ 1 ~

Women were made like
_____;
they were made to be
_____.

~ 2 ~

In this respect, how is a woman a help meet to a man?

~ 3 ~

A. What is the vulnerability
   inherent in a receptacle?

B. What is God's solution
   to this vulnerability?

~ 4 ~

True or False. Marriage will help an individual who is incomplete in her personhood.

~ 5 ~

A. How did satan "plug into" Eve?

B. This has resulted in _____ between femininity and the enemy.

78

~ 6 ~

What must women do because of this conflict with the enemy?

~ 7 ~

How can you tell if something is "plugging into" you or not? Give specific examples.

~ 8 ~

Explain how suffering
and sorrow are part of a
spiritual birth.

~ 9 ~

For every struggle in your life, God accomplished something in your _____ and your _____ .

~ 10 ~

God wants you to _____ the pain and _____ the baby.

~ 11 ~

In the analogy of the birth process, why is it necessary to push?

82

~ 12 ~

What is the balance
that future desire provides?

~ 13 ~

Women of promise are "impregnated with destiny." How does this statement encourage women today?

84

Further Challenge: Take a moment and examine your own life. Do you guard the point of access to your family? What are you allowing entrance into your life and family? Take steps to change what needs changing.

chapter

7

A WOMB-MAN

~ 1 ~

How is the desire to go forward intricately related to the power to create?

~ 2 ~

God wants to give us the strength to...

~ 3 ~

A. Vision is _____
   _____
   _____.

B. Discuss the meaning of vision in light of Proverbs 29:18a.

~ **4** ~

A. What does God use to liberate us?

B. Share some goals that you yourself have.

~ 5 ~

A. What must we put in our spirits to feed, nurture and allow faith to grow?

B. Where do we get this truth? Give some examples.

~ 6 ~

How is faith like money?

~ 7 ~

Describe the way the lives of Abel, Enoch, and Noah present the relationship you can have with God.

~ 8 ~

Does a woman need a man to have vision and faith? Why or why not?

~ 9 ~

Discuss how faith, fear, and God's promises interrelate with each other.

~ 10 ~

A. When a broken person
_____ to God,
God gets the _____
for the wonderful
things He accomplishes.

B. By what means does God
restore you and make you
accomplish great things?

Further Challenge: Look at the relationship Mary and Elisabeth had. What do women today need to do to find similar sister friendships? What can you do to encourage such bonds between yourself and other women? Begin today to cultivate such a friendship.

chapter

8

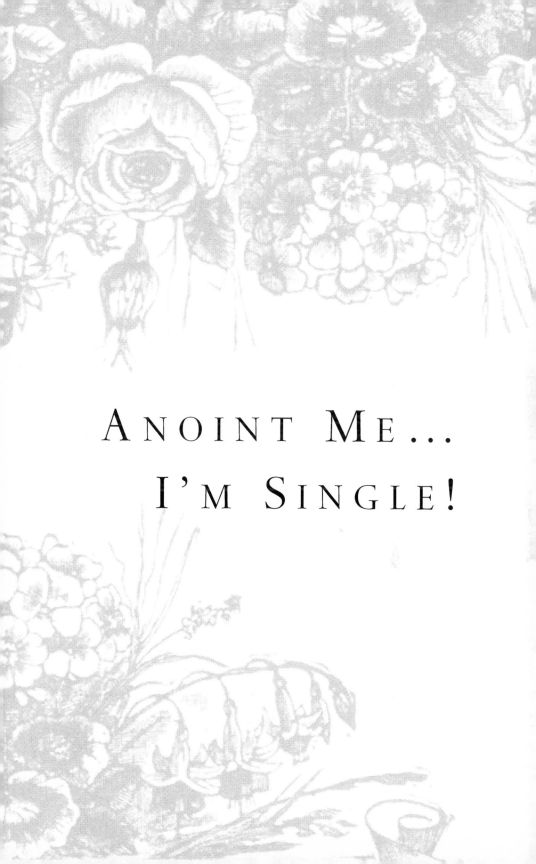

ANOINT ME...
I'M SINGLE!

~ 1 ~

Name some unique
advantages to being single.

~ 2 ~

What should a single person's focus be?

~ 3 ~

List some personal, creative ways you, as a single, can minister to the Lord.

104

~ 4 ~

When you become
faithful in your _____,
then you will be better prepared to be faithful with a

_____:

~ 5 ~

How does God view
singles?

~ 6 ~

Is it wrong for singles to desire companionship? Why or why not?

~ 7 ~

The person who is single should be _____, not _____, in singleness.

~ 8 ~

Discuss some ways in which your relationship with God translates to a relationship with a husband.

~ 9 ~

What is the best example of the sacredness of marriage? Explain.

Further Challenge: If you are single, write a personal and intimate prayer of dedication to the Lord as a husband. Read it aloud to Him, and then sanctify yourself to Him.

chapter

9

A TABLE
FOR TWO

~ 1 ~

What was Adam's attraction to Eve?

~ 2 ~

Explain this statement:
"When it comes to marriage,
no one ever stayed together
simply because they were
attractive."

113

~ 3 ~

A. Everyone needs to pray and discern if their prospective partner is someone they can _____ to the rest of their life.

B. *Debaq,* the Hebrew word for cleave, means: _____

_____.

C. What is the secret to cleaving to a spouse? Discuss fully.

~ 4 ~

How does "The just shall live by faith" (Rom. 1:17b) relate to marriage?

~ 5 ~

A. How is suppressing your own sense of self unhealthy in a relationship?

B. What is the best way to deal with this type of relationship? Use Scripture in your answer.

~ 6 ~

Describe the differences between the communication techniques of men and women.

~ 7 ~

A. List the four points of men's tendency to avoid open confrontation as revealed in Adam's confession.

B. What does a marriage
   need, in order for two
   people to deal with confrontation instead of
   hiding?

~ 8 ~

A. What was it about Delilah that attracted Samson?

B. What can married women learn from Delilah's example?

~ 9 ~

Describe how marriage is a ministry.

121

~ 10 ~

As a married woman, how would you rank your priorities?

122

~ 11 ~

In your own words, describe what it means to be married.

Further Challenge: If you are married, sit down with your spouse and really explore each other's way of communicating. Which ways work best for you? Then begin to practice communicating to bless your spouse.

124

chapter

10

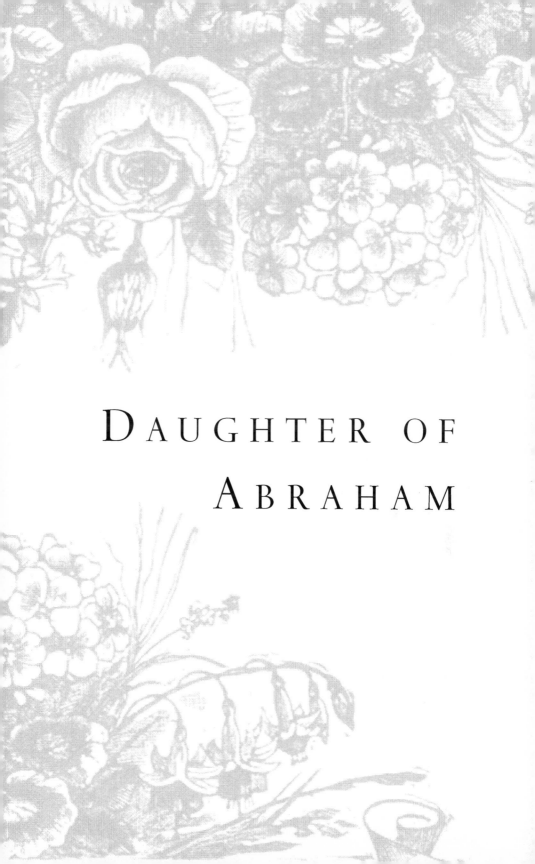

DAUGHTER OF ABRAHAM

~ 1 ~

Many see Jesus as a way to Heaven and the solution to _____ problems, but they fail to see that He is the solution to _____ problems.

~ 2 ~

Name some areas (other than spiritual) in which Jesus is our solution.

~ 3 ~

A. How much are we to
   want Jesus?

B. What does that show
   about a person?

~ 4 ~

No matter what the problem is, _____ is the answer.

~ 5 ~

From the moment you are called to Jesus, you become _____:

~ 6 ~

What can ensnare us and hinder us from becoming whole?

130

~ 7 ~

Jesus' power showed how powerless His critics' _____ was.

~ 8 ~

What must our ambition be?

~ 9 ~

A. Our _____ should not negate our _____.

B. What is your position today? Whose are you?

~ 10 ~

Does gender matter when a person approaches God? Why or why not?

~ 11 ~

A. Faith is more than a
_____ —faith
is an _____.

B. Choose two people from
the "faith hall of fame" in
Hebrews 11 and describe
their faith. How was their
faith an action?

~ 12 ~

Faith is what _____ God.

~ 13 ~

If you want the enemy to release you, _____

_____

_____.

~ 14 ~

What must you do to receive what has been left to you?

~ 15 ~

True or False. It is what you say about yourself, and what God has said about you, that really matters.

~ 16 ~

Faith is the only thing in this world where there is...

Further Challenge: Are your words crippling you or loosing you? Take the time today to think about each thing you say—no matter who you talk to. What are you saying as you converse with your co-workers? Your friends? Your children? Your spouse? Correct whatever comes from your mouth that does not reflect your position as a child of the heavenly Father. Begin to speak deliverance and power.

137

chapter

11

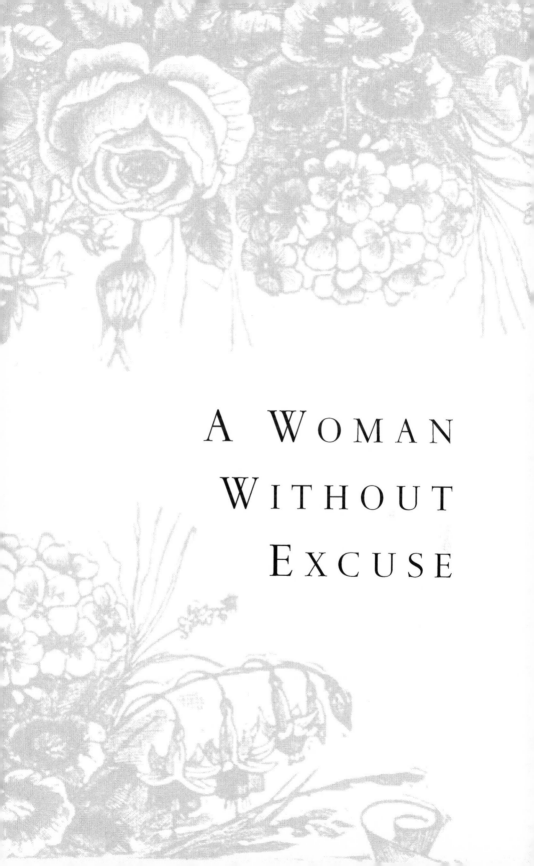

A WOMAN WITHOUT EXCUSE

~ 1 ~

A. How do attitudes affect your life?

B. An attitude results from

_____

_____ .

C. Explain what perspective is.

~ 2 ~

We need to learn how to _____ _____ our perspective and _____ our attitudes.

~ 3 ~

True or False. People are supposed to function in life under the burdens of pressure.

~ 4 ~

How can a problem be an excuse? Share a personal example.

~ 5 ~

Before you can get out of trouble, you need to...

~ 6 ~

One of the greatest deliverances people can ever experience in life is...

~ 7 ~

Healing attitudes set people free to receive

_____.

~ 8 ~

A. How can you protect yourself from accusers and negativism?

B. What must you do to allow the Lord to fight for you?

~ **9** ~

A. Love is _____.
It is not limited by
_____.

B. How does this concern
marriage relationships?

144

~ 10 ~

How can the Church help the wounded?

Further Challenge: List some ways you can help change your attitude. Then ask the Holy Spirit for His help in reminding you about your attitude when you find yourself getting angry or depressed. When He does, stop and change your attitude.

146

chapter

12

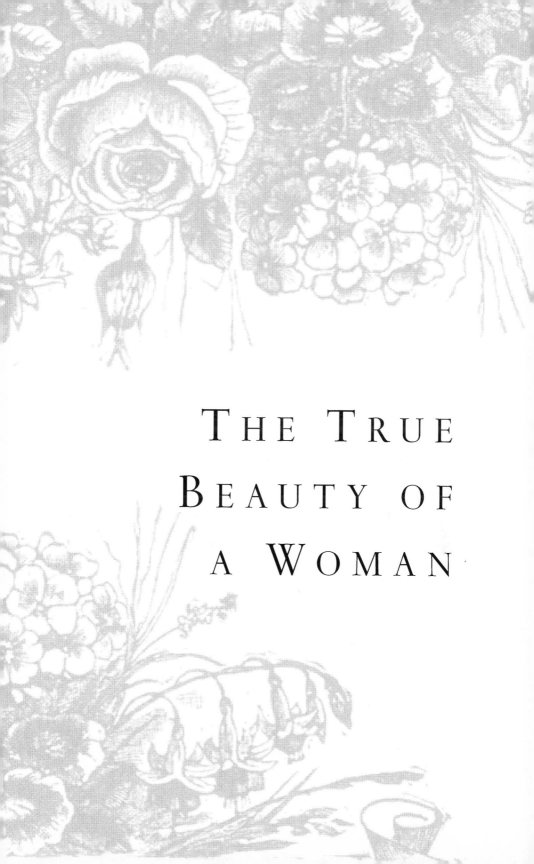

THE TRUE
BEAUTY OF
A WOMAN

150

~ 1 ~

We must learn to _____ God for who we are. We must start _____ ourselves.

~ 2 ~

God put some things into the feminine _____ that a man needs more than anything God put on the feminine _____.

~ 3 ~

What does a woman need to know to be attractive to a man?

~ 4 ~

God has adorned the woman _____.

~ 5 ~

According to First Peter 3:1, to whom should a woman be in subjection?

~ **6** ~

A. What does the word *conversation* in First Peter 3:1 refer to?

B. Why is this important in a marriage relationship?

~ 7 ~

What did Delilah give Samson that kept him coming back?

~ 8 ~

What valuable ornament did God give to women?

~ 9 ~

True or False. Sexual ability is more powerful than a meek and quiet spirit.

~ 10 ~

When are women daughters of Sarah?

~ 11 ~

True beauty is always…

Further Challenge: Do you know anything about painting and artwork? Find out how an artist goes about producing a master-piece—how much time and care does he or she put into that one piece? Then consider how much more God has produced a work of art in you.

13

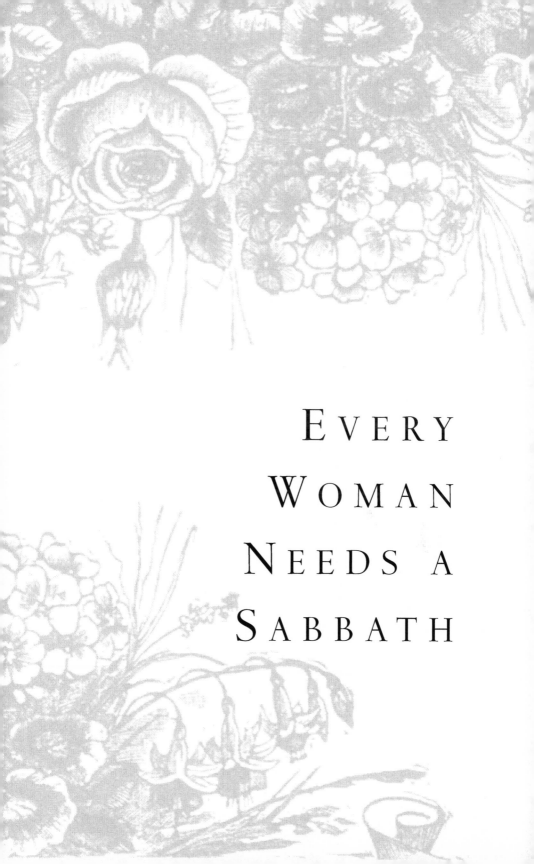

EVERY WOMAN NEEDS A SABBATH

~ 1 ~

The Sabbath is a day of
_____. It is a day of
_____.

~ 2 ~

It is during a time of
rest that you...

~ 3 ~

Why do you need to
rest your spirit?

~ **4** ~

**What is another pur-
pose for the Sabbath?**

~ 5 ~

When is the best time to have God minister to your needs?

~ **6** ~

Describe some times of rest and God's refreshing that you have experienced in your own life.

164

~ 7 ~

. Our Sabbath rest is

_____ .

~ 8 ~

A. True or False. The enemy
    prefers seeing you at rest.

B. Justify your answer.

~ 9 ~

Discuss how the perspective of the woman at the well changed from anxiety to peace.

~ 10 ~

When you get the
_____, it gives
you the _____ to
let go of the _____.

~ 11 ~

The Sabbath rest is the
_____ to find

in _____.

Further Challenge:
Having a specific time to
rest and restore your spirit
in the Lord is important for
your spiritual health.
Choose a time in your day
when you won't be dis-
tracted and worship the
Lord. Be willing to sacrifice
to find this time and to
make it a habit. The reward
is well worth the effort.

chapter

14

WINTER
WOMAN

~ 1 ~

Describe the beauty you see in each season, as it relates to the life span of a woman:

A. Spring

B. Summer

C. Autumn

D. Winter

~ 2 ~

It is important that we teach women to prepare for

_____.

~ 3 ~

Why should we spend more time encouraging older women?

172

~ 4 ~

Just because demands have _____ doesn't mean life is _____.

~ 5 ~

God tends to save the _____ for _____.

~ 6 ~

A. How did God restore purpose to Naomi's life?

B. What do you think would have happened if Naomi had persisted in being depressed and bitter?

173

~ 7 ~

What other relationships are there besides family ones?

174

~ 8 ~

Describe the bonds between:

A. Naomi and Ruth.

B. Elisabeth and Mary.

~ 9 ~

There are two things every winter woman, every Naomi, can rely upon:

A. God is a _____.
   What does this mean?

B. God will be known as the _____. What does this mean?

~ 10 ~

Angels are the _____
of Heaven.

~ 11 ~

What is the purpose
of angels? Explain using
Scripture.

~ 12 ~

In a few sentences, describe the process Sarah went through from hearing God's promise to receiving the promise.

~ 13 ~

What did Sarah learn
that all of us must learn too?

~ 14 ~

An example to women in every season of life, how is Sarah an example to you in your season?

Further Challenge: Look back to the friendship between Naomi and Ruth. If you are a winter woman, what are some things you can do to help younger women? What do you know from your life's experience that you can pass to others? Ask God to reveal to you His purpose for you as a winter woman.

chapter

15

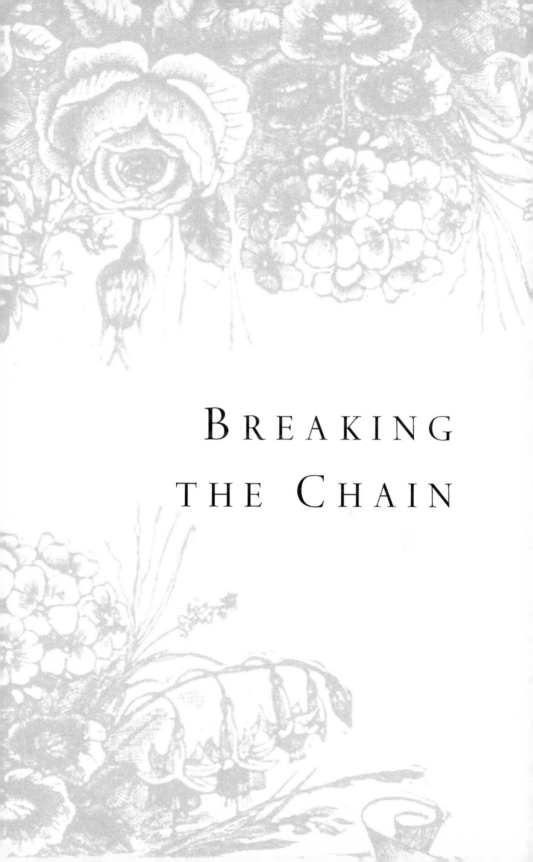

BREAKING
THE CHAIN

~ 1 ~

A. Why has the enemy con-
   centrated on destroying
   women?

B. What does this response
   say to your heart?

~ 2 ~

What has God done to
meet your need?

~ 3 ~

Is there anything too great for the grace of God to forgive?

~ 4 ~

What happens when we
accept Jesus as our Savior?

~ 5 ~

If the past is paid for,
why then do we have scars?

188

~ 6 ~

God recognizes the
_____ of what
you can _____. He
has a _____. He sees
your _____.

~ 7 ~

What does God want to
set free?

~ 8 ~

What can you do to respond to His call and be freed?

Truly, you can do all things through Christ who strengthens you. Woman, be thou loosed!

ANSWER KEY

CHAPTER ONE

1. A. 1. the person

    2. the problem

    3. the prescription

    B. For every person there will be a problem; and for every problem, God has a prescription.

2. A present word from God. God's Word, Jesus, is timeless; according to Hebrews 13:8, He is the same yesterday, today, and forever.

3. Reader's discussion.

4. True

5. A. As a narcotic to numb the pain.

   B. It does not allow God to heal a person; it can become addictive.

6. False

7. Spirit of infirmity

8. ...forgiveness

9. Personal response.

10. By renewing her mind through the Word of God.

11. Reader's discussion.

12. Reader's discussion.

13. A. ...receiver

    B. Women must be careful what they receive; they must not allow the enemy to "plug into" their lives. They must receive only what agrees with the Word of God.

14. Forgetting is more than not remembering; it is letting go of the memory.

CHAPTER TWO

1. For their abilities and potential for the future; for going where their parents point them.

2. Personal response.

3. A. ...the mother of miracles.

B. Compassion allows healing power to flow; many
times in Jesus' ministry His compassion preceded
the healing (Mt. 9:36; 14:14; 18:27; Mk. 1:41; 6:34).

4. No. It affects the inside of a person, not the outside.

5. Personal response.

6. A. He stopped teaching, held them, touched them,
and blessed them.

B. Personal response.

7. A. ...God giving us a chance to start over again.

B. Personal response.

8. Personal response.

9. Personal response.

10. A. To be uncovered is to be unprotected.

B. With the blood of Jesus Christ.

11. ... intensive care

12. Personal response.

CHAPTER THREE

1. Personal response.

2. The flesh.

3. By receiving it by faith, and by allowing the blood
of Jesus to sanctify the innermost being.

4. The Church is like a hospital that cares for people while they are in the process of becoming whole again.

5. A. Matthew was a tax collector who most likely gained his wealth by charging exorbitant taxes. Mary Magdalene was a prostitute. (Reader may have other examples.)

   B. Personal response.

6. demarcation; past; present

7. He understood the need to meet people where they were and to minister to their need.

8. ...from events that we have no control over.

9. ...living lives that bring bondage and pain.

10. A. forgive

    B. heal

    C. restore

11. The potential of their future.

CHAPTER FOUR

1. David's weakness was a passion for women; his son Amnon also exhibited this passion. Personal response.

2. Love is a giving force; lust is a selfish compulsion focused on gratifying self.

3. Complete healing—in spirit, emotions (mind), and body.

4. A. Their maternal instinct; also, a need for love.

   B. By exercising discernment.

5. True

6. Through a relationship with God as Father; also through platonic relationships with men.

7. nurture; protect

8. Personal response.

9. A. The ability to open your past to someone responsible enough to share your weaknesses and pains.

   B. Believers can listen to and help one another in their weaknesses, according to Galatians 6:2.

   C. Personal response.

CHAPTER FIVE

1. Personal response.

2. He did not want her.

3. "I want you."

4. He called her forward, waited for her to reach Him, then proclaimed her freedom.

5. Personal response.

6. power; anointing

7. Joy.

8. Physical (platonic) touch; the Word of God; spiritual food; atmosphere of sharing and acceptance.

9. A. 1. historical faith

   2. futuristic faith

   3. present faith
      Personal response.

   B. Present faith. It is current.

CHAPTER SIX

1. receptacles; receivers

2. She is the receptacle he plugs into so he can meet and accomplish his task.

3. A. It is open to be plugged into.

   B. The commitment of the marriage covenant.

4. False

5. A. He took advantage of her desire to see, taste and be wise; he caught her attention; he deceived her.

   B. enmity *or* conflict

6. They must do spiritual warfare.

7. By being vulnerable to moods, attitudes and dis-
   positions; by doing things and not knowing why
   (for example, "I just feel like doing this").

8. Suffering and sorrow are the way through which a
   spiritual baby is born.

9. character; spirit

10. drop; hold

11. A baby will not come unless there is pushing; it is
    necessary to push in order to produce.

12. It gives the incentive to be productive again after
    the pain.

13. It gives a sense of worth and purpose.

CHAPTER SEVEN

1. It is when the desire to go forward is greater than
   the memories of pain that a person has the power
   to create again.

2. ...overcome past pain and move forward into new
   life.

3. A. ...the desire to go ahead.

   B. Reader's discussion.

4. A. A goal.

   B. Personal response.

5. A. Truth.

B. The Word of God. Deuteronomy 28:13; Psalm 8:3-4; 139:14; Philippians 4:13; etc.

6. It is the means, the tender, by which you receive the things you hope for.

7. Abel worshiped God by faith; Enoch walked with God by faith; Noah worked with God by faith. Worshiping comes before walking, and walking before working.

8. No. She herself can have faith; each person needs his or her own walk with God.

9. Reader's discussion.

10. A. submits; glory

B. His anointing.

CHAPTER EIGHT

1. A single woman can serve God with more freedom; she can pray, praise and worship God whenever and however she wants; she can build herself up in the Lord without other distractions.

2. The Lord and her relationship with Him.

3. Personal response.

4. singleness; husband

5. As belonging to Him.

6. No. It is a God-ordained need.

7. abiding; wrestling

8. Reader's discussion.

9. The relationship between Jesus and the Church. Jesus is the greatest advocate and intercessor for believers.

CHAPTER NINE

1. Her likeness to him.

2. A commitment requires an attraction that is deeper than outward appearance.

3. A. cleave

   B. "to impinge, cling or adhere to; figuratively, to catch by pursuit or follow close after"

   C. The secret to cleaving is leaving. Reader's discussion.

4. It is through faith that a marriage relationship can be changed.

5. A. It can lead to depression and will not guarantee an end to being hurt.

   B. To show by lifestyle, according to First Peter 3:1-2, the purity and reverence in your life.

6. Men tend to be physical and women tend to be vocal.

7. A. 1. Adam heard God's voice.

2. Adam was afraid.

3. Adam was naked.

4. Adam hid himself.

B. The ability to be transparent; to expose vulnerabilities without fear or condemnation.

8. A. She gave him rest and cared for him.

B. How to treat men like little boys, to give rest, to give safety, to praise, etc.

9. When you marry a person, you marry all of his past, his weaknesses, strengths, fears, etc. The things that need healing, you can minister to.

10. Personal response.

11. Personal response.

CHAPTER TEN

1. spiritual; all of life's

2. Finances, emotions, self-esteem, etc.

3. A. We are to want Him enough to overcome obstacles and to push in His direction.

B. It shows how much they want help.

4. Jesus

5. ...invincible

6. Our own words.

7. religion

8. Jesus Christ.

9. A. condition; position

   B. Personal response.

10. No. There is no discrimination in faith.

11. A. fact; action

    B. Personal response.

12. moves

13. ...remind him whose daughter you are.

14. You must ask for it; you must speak correctly.

15. True

16. ...true equal opportunity.

CHAPTER ELEVEN

1. A. A good attitude can bring success; a poor attitude can bring destruction.

   B. ...perspective

   C. Perspective is the way people look at life, which is often determined by their history.

2. look past; change

3. False

4. A problem can become a reason not to do other things, a reason for not changing. Personal response.

5. ...straighten out your attitude.

6. ...to have their attitude delivered.

7. ...wholeness

8. A. By praising God, and not stopping.

   B. Quit defending yourself and attacking others.

9. A. eternal; time

   B. When you love your partner, your love covers everything—including his history and how it makes him react to certain things.

10. By sharing burdens, trusting one another, pointing to God, providing a haven of praise.

CHAPTER TWELVE

1. thank; appreciating

2. spirit; body

3. To know who she is on the inside; to know her own self-worth.

4. ...inwardly

5. Her own husband.

6. A. Lifestyle.

    B. Unbelieving husbands watch their wives for their attitudes, dispositions, and words.

7. Rest.

8. A meek and quiet spirit.

9. False

10. When they are not afraid, remain calm, keep control, rebuke fear, trust in God, judge God faithful, smile through tears, etc.

11. ...on the inside.

CHAPTER THIRTEEN

1. rest; restoration

2. ...replenish or receive back those things that were expended or put out.

3. It is through rest that your life can begin to be restored.

4. For communion with God.

5. When in real worship.

6. Personal response.

7. ...Christ Jesus.

8. A. False

B. He would rather break up your rest to keep you from being restored.

9. Reader's discussion.

10. rest; power; anxiety

11. ability; eternal satisfaction; Jesus

CHAPTER FOURTEEN

1. Personal repsonse.

2. ...winter

3. When they lose the people they built their lives around, they feel displaced and need new roles.

4. changed; over

5. best; last

6. A. He gave her a relationship with Ruth.

   B. Personal response.

7. Friendships; "God-bonds."

8. Personal response.

9. A. ...restorer; He restores purpose to the past and He makes up for the toll the past took on a person.

   B. ...nourisher; He will care for and supply the needs of those who used to care for and supply the needs of others.

10. butlers

11. They are to minister to God's people, according to Hebrews 1:14. (Other explanations are possible.)

12. Personal response.

13. The faithfulness of God.

14. Personal response.

CHAPTER FIFTEEN

1. A. They are God's vehicles of creativity.

   B. Personal response.

2. He sent a Redeemer, Jesus Christ.

3. No.

4. We are made pure; we become clean and holy.

5. Scars remind us that we are human.

6. possibility; become; plan; potential

7. The woman inside who can do great exploits in His name.

8. Have faith. Believe He will do what He said He would. Put your confidence in His power. Trust in Him.

Believe He has washed you and made you clean. Believe He will satisfy every need.

Made in the USA
Monee, IL
18 May 2020